DEPARTMENT OF THE NAVY
HEADQUARTERS UNITED STATES MARINE CORPS
3000 MARINE CORPS PENTAGON
WASHINGTON, DC 20350-3000

MCO P11000.5G
LFF-2
30 Sep 04

MARINE CORPS ORDER P11000.5G W/CH 1

From: Commandant of the Marine Corps

To: Distribution List

Subj: REAL PROPERTY FACILITIES MANUAL, VOLUME IV, FACILITIES PROJECTS MANUAL

Ref: (a) MCO P11000.3B

Encl: (1) Locator Sheet

1. <u>Situation</u>. The Marine Corps owns significant quantities of real property facilities and assets. Sustaining these real property facilities and assets are critical to mission accomplishment, quality of service and quality of life.

2. <u>Cancellation</u>. MCO P11000.5F

3. <u>Mission</u>. This order provides guidance and instruction as related to facilities projects.

4. <u>Execution</u>

   a. <u>Commander's Intent and Concept of Operations</u>

      (1) This Manual, while providing guidance, allows the installation commander flexibility in administering the facilities project program. Requirements and policy are clearly defined in this Manual. Additional information, details and examples are provided on K21 (https://K21.hqmc.usmc.mil).

      (2) Installation commanders will review this Manual, and ensure that they are in compliance.

5. <u>Administration and Logistics</u>

   a. Recommendations regarding improvements concerning the contents of this Manual are encouraged and should be submitted to the Commandant of the Marine Corps (CMC) (LFF-2) via the appropriate chain of command.

DISTRIBUTION STATEMENT A: Approved for public release; distribution is unlimited.

   b. <u>Command</u>. The Manual is not applicable to Marine Corps
Reserve components except as indicated in the reference.

6. <u>Certification</u>. Reviewed and approved this date.

DISTRIBUTION: PCN 10211280000

   Copy to: 7000260 (2)
             7000162 (5)
             7000144/8145001 (1)

DEPARTMENT OF THE NAVY
HEADQUARTERS UNITED STATES MARINE CORPS
3000 MARINE CORPS PENTAGON
WASHINGTON, DC 20350-3000

MCO P11000.5G Ch 1
LFF-2
01 AUG 2007

MARINE CORPS ORDER P11000.5G Ch 1

From: Commandant of the Marine Corps
To: Distribution List

Subj: REAL PROPERTY FACILITIES MANUAL, VOLUME IV, FACILITIES PROJECTS
       MANUAL CHANGE 1

Encl: (1) New page inserts to MCO P11000.5G

1. Situation. To transmit new page inserts to the basic Order.

2. Mission. This change updates Marine Corps policy on the demolition of existing Marine Corps owned facilities in conjunction with repair and minor construction projects. This change also gives clear cut guidance on mandating the installation of fire sprinkler systems when the repair cost is less than 50% of the replacement cost of the facility.

3. Execution

    a. Remove the overall table of contents, page iii. Replace with the corresponding page iii in enclosure (1).

    b. Remove pages 2-17 through 2-21. Replace with corresponding pages 2-17 through 2-20 in enclosure (1).

    c. Remove page 3-1. Replace with corresponding page 3-1 in enclosure (1).

    d. Remove pages 3-9 through 3-11. Replace with the corresponding pages 3-9 through 3-11 in enclosure (1).

    e. Remove pages 4-1 and 4-2. Replace with corresponding pages 4-1 and 4-2 in enclosure (1).

    f. Remove pages 4-5 and 4-7. Replace with corresponding pages 4-5 and 4-7 in enclosure (1).

4. Filing Instructions. File this change transmittal page in front of the original Order.

R. S. KRAMLICH
Deputy Commandant for
Installations and Logistics

DISTRIBUTION STATEMENT A: Approved for public release; distribution is unlimited.

DISTRIBUTION: PCN 10211280001

   Copy to: 7000162(25)
              7000093,144/8145004,005 (2)
              7000260/8145001 (1)

LOCATOR SHEET

Subj: REAL PROPERTY FACILITIES MANUAL

Location: _____
            Indicate the location(s) of the copy(ies) of this Manual).

REAL PROPERTY FACILITIES MANUAL

RECORD OF CHANGES

Log completed change action as indicated.

Change Number	Date of Change	Date Entered	Signature of Person Incorporated Change

REAL PROPERTY FACILITIES MANUAL

CONTENTS

REAL PROPERTY FACILITIES MANUAL

CHAPTER 1

INTRODUCTION

CHAPTER 1

INTRODUCTION

1000. PURPOSE. Facilities projects are prepared in support of each activity's mission and to meet the Marine Corps' goals. Congressional interest in the proper and effective use of program resources makes the classification of work in facilities projects very important. This Manual provides policy and guidance for the preparation, submission, review, approval, and reporting of facilities projects at Marine Corps installations.

1001. POLICY

1. Operation, sustainment, restoration, and modernization of Marine Corps real property shall be:

   a. Consistent with law, Congressional guidance, Department of Defense (DoD) policy, Department of Navy (DON), and Marine Corps guidance.

   b. In direct support of mission requirements.

   c. Performed in full consideration of total life-cycle costs.

   d. Accomplished through the most economic means.

2. Congress established restrictions on the use of appropriated funds in the following laws:

   a. Title 31 U.S.C. 1301(A) - requires that appropriated funds be used only for the programs and purposes for which the appropriation is approved.

   b. Title 31 U.S.C. 1517 - prohibits authorizing an obligation more than the amount available in an appropriation or permitted by agency regulations.

3. For issues not specifically covered by this Manual, refer to OPNAVINST 11010.20 for information.

1002. CONTENT

1. Facilities projects involve work on real property. This Manual addresses the various classifications of facilities projects and the associated documentation and processing requirements. The classifications of facilities projects are:

    a. Sustainment (chapter 3) - Includes maintenance and most repair work.

    b. Restoration and Modernization (chapter 4) - Includes specific repair work that meets the definition of restoration and all construction work.

    c. Equipment Installation (chapter 5).

2. This manual deals exclusively with Operation and Maintenance, Marine Corps (O&MMC) funded work. Excluded from the provisions of this Manual are:

    a. Projects funded solely from appropriations for procurement that do not include work classified as construction.

    b. Projects funded with appropriations for the Marine Corps Reserve. Marine Forces Reserves (MARFORRES) MCO P11000R.20 contains applicable information on Marine Corps Reserve projects.

    c. Projects funded from appropriations for family housing construction and maintenance. MCO P11000.22 contains applicable information on family housing projects.

    d. Projects funded from non-appropriated funds (NAF). MCO P11000.12 and MCO P1700.27 contain applicable information on NAF projects.

   e. Projects authorized by Title 10 U.S.C. 2353 and funded
from Research, Development, Test, and Evaluation (RDT&E)
appropriations for facilities and equipment provided to a
contractor.

   f. Projects solely for the acquisition of real estate
(class 1 property). See Naval Facilities Engineering Command
(NAVFAC) Publication, NAVFAC P-73 for applicable information on
real estate acquisition.

   g. Projects funded with appropriations from governments
other than the United States of America. MCO P11000.12 contains
applicable information on projects funded with appropriations
from governments other than the United States of America.

   h. Projects funded with private funds. MCO P11000.12
contains applicable information on privately funded projects.

   i. Projects financed from the Environmental Restoration,
Navy (ERN) appropriation. MCO P5090.2 contains applicable
information on ERN projects.

   j. Projects funded by Navy Working Capital Fund (NWCF)
entities.

   k. Projects funded from appropriations of the Military
Construction (MILCON) Appropriation. MCO P11000.12 contains
applicable information on MILCON projects.

1003. SUMMARY OF REVISION. This Manual has been reformatted
and contains major and administrative changes. The major
modifications to this Manual are as follow:

1. Chapter 1. Creates a listing of responsibilities for the
CMC; Commander, Marine Forces, Atlantic (COMMARFORLANT);
Commander, Marine Forces, Pacific (COMMARFORPAC); and Commander,
Marine Corps Logistics Command (COMMARCORLOGCOM).

2. Chapter 2. Updates a listing of major and minor Marine Corps installations. Updates a listing of Special Programs and inserts section about the Marine Corps Demolition Program. Includes a change to the project numbering system for environmental projects. Limits projects to one facility and utility per project. Implements the new requirement for Assistant Secretary of the Navy (Installations & Environment) (ASN (I&E)) approval of repair projects costing more than $5 million.

3. Chapter 3. Provides the definition of sustainment. Describes how maintenance and repair relate to sustainment. Updates the definition of "repair" to allow for the performance of modifications and additions to comply with national or regional building code, or environmental regulations.

4. Chapter 4. Provides the definition of Restoration and Modernization. Describes the four criteria that, if met, classifies repair work as restoration and modernization. Requires that improvements to multiple real property facilities, for the same mission requirement, purpose and category code, must be considered a single undertaking. Adds criteria that must be met when accomplishing multiple minor construction projects in the same real property facility. Includes the policy raising the statutory O&MMC minor construction limit to $750,000 for regular minor construction projects, and to $1.5 million for minor construction projects performed solely for life, health, or safety threatening conditions. Limits repair cost for a project to 75 percent of plant replacement value. Adds section on construction in other than Marine Corps-owned facilities.

5. Chapter 5. Provides classifications for equipment installation projects. Disseminates policy regarding maintenance and repair of interior and exterior telecommunications systems.

1004. RESPONSIBILITIES

1. Commanders of Marine Corps installations shall comply with the contents of this Manual. Specifically, they shall:

a. Ensure that work descriptions, justifications, impacts, cost estimates, and drawings in all project documentation are complete, current, and accurate.

b. Ensure statutory limits are not exceeded and maintain complete, current, accurate and auditable records of program execution on actual project expenditures and changes to project scope and contracts.

c. Coordinate all project costs (to include associated unfunded costs, such as collateral equipment and telecommunications).

d. Obtain all required authorizations, approvals, clearances, permits, and funds (or funding commitment) before initiating any project procurement action.

e. Use program funds only as authorized by the CMC.

f. Review unprogrammed and emergent project requirements to verify their necessity, urgency, and lack of local funding, if within local commander's authority, before submitting them to the CMC.

g. Develop and execute projects in a timely and effective manner to fulfill program targets and goals. This includes the coordination of other associated costs, approval, and funding requirements for the project.

2. The COMMARFORLANT, COMMARFORPAC, and COMMARLOGCOM have a role in the projects program to distribute funds provided from the CMC to the installations under their cognizance. Specifically, they shall:

a. Provide timely flow of funds from the CMC to installations under their cognizance for contract award of special projects.

     b. Distribute the full amount of lump-sum design funds
provided by the CMC to installations under their cognizance.

     c. Coordinate timely requests for and distribution of
change order funds from the CMC to installations under their
cognizance. Ensure local sources of funds, including the
COMMARFORLANT, COMMARFORPAC, and COMMARCORLOGCOM levels, have
been fully exhausted prior to requesting "within contingency"
change orders.

     d. Provide liaison support as required between the
CMC (LFF) and the bases and stations under their cognizance.

3. The CMC (LFF) provides funding, central direction and
oversight concerning the maintenance of real property
facilities. Specifically, they shall:

     a. Field validate major repair, and minor construction
projects.

     b. Evaluate relative need and proper classification of all
projects to ensure consistency and adherence to statutory limits
and regulations.

     c. Authorize design and contact award for projects above
the local commander's authority based on relative need and
funding levels.

     d. Establish authorized cost for projects based on DD 1391s
and other documentation provided by the installations.

     e. Distribute funds for design and contract award on time.

     f. Evaluate and coordinate requests for and distribution of
change order funds above the project's authorized cost.

1005. ACRONYMS. A list of acronyms appearing in this Manual is
located at appendix A.

REAL PROPERTY FACILITIES MANUAL

CHAPTER 2

PROCEDURES FOR FACILITIES PROJECTS

REAL PROPERTY FACILITIES MANUAL

CHAPTER 2

PROCEDURES FOR FACILITIES PROJECTS

SECTION 1: GENERAL INFORMATION

2100. <u>TERMS APPLICABLE TO PROJECTS</u>. The following terms and definitions apply to this Manual.

1. <u>Project</u>. A single planned undertaking of sustainment, or restoration and modernization, performed on a single facility, to satisfy a finite work requirement.

2. <u>Real Property</u>. Land and all facilities added to the land for which the U.S. Government has right, title, or interest.

3. <u>Facility</u>. A facility is a separate building, structure, or other improvement to real property.

4. <u>Installation</u>. An installation is categorized mainly by the overall physical size into either a major or minor installation. For the purposes of this manual, there are nineteen major installations and seven minor installations within the Marine Corps as follows:

   a. <u>Minor Installations</u>

        (1) Headquarters Battalion, Henderson Hall, Arlington, Virginia

        (2) Marine Barracks, 8th and I Streets, SE, Washington, DC

        (3) Camp Allen, Norfolk, Virginia

        (4) 1st Marine Corps District, Garden City, New York

        (5) Marine Corps Support Activity, Kansas City, Missouri

      (6) Mountain Warfare Training Center (MWTC), Bridgeport, California

      (7) Blount Island Command, Jacksonville, Florida

  b. <u>Major Installations</u>

      (1) Marine Corps Logistics Base (MCLB) Albany, Georia

      (2) MCLB Barstow, California

      (3) Marine Corps Air Station (MCAS) Beaufort, South Carolina

      (4) Marine Corps Base (MCB) Camp Butler, Japan

      (5) MCAS Cherry Point, North Carolina

      (6) MCAS Futenma, Japan

      (7) MCB Hawaii, Kaneohe Bay, Hawaii

      (8) MCAS Iwakuni, Japan

      (9) MCB Camp Lejeune, North Carolina

      (10) MCAS Miramar, California

      (11) MCAS New River, North Carolina

      (12) Marine Corps Recruit Depot (MCRD)/Eastern Recruiting Region Parris Island, South Carolina

      (13) MCB Camp Pendleton, California

      (14) MCAS Camp Pendleton, California

      (15) MCB Quantico, Virginia

      (16) Marine Corps Air Facility (MCAF) Quantico, Virginia

      (17) MCRD/Western Recruiting Region San Diego, California

      (18) Marine Air-Ground Task Force Training Command (MAGTFTC) Twentynine Palms, California

      (19) MCAS Yuma, Arizona

5. Installation Commander. A commanding officer (CO), or equivalent, of an installation having fixed boundaries within which all persons are subject to the military jurisdiction and the authority of the CO.

6. Category Code. A five-digit system of numbering a common nomenclature for classes 1 and 2 plant property. See NAVFAC P-72, Department of the Navy Facility Category Codes, for a listing of recognized codes.

7. DoD Facilities Analysis Code (FAC). A four-digit system of numbering a common nomenclature for class 2 plant property. See the current DoD Cost Factors Handbook for a listing of DoD standard codes.

8. Supervision, Inspection and Overhead (SIOH) and Contract Administration. These are costs charged by NAVFAC for support associated with the administration of contracts for facilities projects.

9. NWCF. A working capital fund used to fund the operations of specified support activities. NWCF entities are to budget and fund sustainment, and restoration and modernization requirements in facilities they own, have exclusive use of, or occupy.

10. Funded Project Cost. Costs used when determining who holds approval authority for a facilities project. Funded project costs for facilities projects include the following:

    a. Labor. Labor costs for in-house civilian employees are calculated based upon guidance in the FMB Manual, volume 3, chapter 5, paragraph 035030, or volume 5, part J, chapter 4, section IV, as appropriate. When the work is accomplished by contract, include the labor component of all contract costs except architectural and engineering (A&E) fees. Military labor is not a funded cost.

b. Material. The cost of direct material (government or contractor furnished) used in accomplishing the project.

c. Equipment. The cost of all built-in equipment (government or contractor furnished). See paragraph 5100.1 for the definition of "built-in" equipment.

d. Land. The cost of land for the proposed project only if acquired under the authority of Title 10 U.S.C. 2673.

e. Overhead. The portion of activity operations or support that represents additional costs and would not have been incurred were it not for the project (e.g.: administration or inspection of the construction). Contractor overhead and profit is a funded cost. Government SIOH and contract administration as identified in NAVFACINST 7820.1H are funded costs.

f. Transportation. The costs applicable to transportation of rented and government-owned materials and supplies. Projects accomplished by Military Construction Forces shall include these costs only when a deployment is intended for the sole purpose of accomplishing a particular project. The cost of transportation of materials transferred between supply offices is not included as a funded project cost.

g. Surplus stock. Cost of materials, supplies, and items of installed equipment obtained from surplus stocks within the Navy or Marine Corps. Pricing of the property must be equal to that charged by the surplus stock manager or at the estimated fair market value.

h. Travel and Per Diem. The cost of travel and per diem applicable to military labor is a funded project cost only when a deployment is intended for the sole purpose of accomplishing a particular project.

    i. <u>Construction equipment</u>. Costs applicable to O&M of rented and government-owned equipment used in the execution of a project.

11. <u>Unfunded Project Costs</u>. Costs excluded when determining who holds approval authority for a facilities project. Unfunded project costs for facilities projects include the following:

    a. <u>Military labor</u>. All costs financed from Military Personnel Appropriations.

    b. <u>Equipment Depreciation</u>. Costs applicable to the depreciation of government-owned equipment.

    c. <u>Surplus Stock from Outside the Navy or Marine Corps</u>. Cost of materials, supplies, and items of installed equipment obtained for a project from sources outside the Navy or Marine Corps (e.g., excess distributions from other government agencies).

    d. <u>Planning and Design</u>. Costs associated with preparation of design plans and specifications (A&E contracts and in-house design costs) and costs to develop Operation and Maintenance Support Information products for specific projects. However, in design-build contracts, the cost of design is part of the project funded cost.

    e. <u>Professional Services</u>. Costs associated with engineering services (e.g., soil boring, surveys, inspections, and various types of testing and analyses).

    f. <u>Personal Property</u>. Items bought from appropriations for procurement (e.g., classes 3 and 4 plant property (see paragraph 2103 of this Manual)).

12. <u>Current Working Estimate (CWE)</u>. The CWE is the government cost estimate for a specific project. It is the sum of all funded costs.

13. Authorized Cost. The authorized cost is the amount
approved by the CMC for execution of a specific project. It
includes the project total funded costs and any contingency
ceiling provided by the CMC.

14. Plant Replacement Value (PRV). The cost to construct a
replacement facility using current building codes, design
criteria, and materials. The PRV is calculated from the size of
the current facility, published DoD unit costs for that type of
facility, the local area cost factor, design, contingency, and
SIOH.

2101. PROGRAM SCOPE AND LIMITATION(S)

1. Headquarters Marine Corps (HQMC) Facilities Projects
Program. The HQMC Facilities Projects Program is a centrally
managed, interrelated program for developing, prioritizing and
funding sustainment, and restoration and modernization projects
at Marine Corps installations. Operation of the program in
detailed in chapter 2, sections 2, 3, and 4 of this Manual.

2. Limits of Authority. Approval authority limits for
O&MMC funded facilities projects at HQMC and Marine Corps
installations are listed in appendix B. The dollar amounts
listed are total funded project cost.

2102. FUND SOURCES. Facilities projects are financed from one
of three broad categories of funding sources.

1. Appropriated Funds. The Congress through specific
legislation provides appropriated funds. Examples include
MILCON appropriations, O&M appropriations, and appropriations
for procurement.

2. NAF. NAF consist of cash and/or other assets received from
sources other than that appropriated by Congress. Examples
include revenues generated from retail sales, private funds

received from non-government entities, and public funds from governments other than the United States of America.

3. <u>NWCF</u>. Working capital funds are generated locally through the sale of products and services (generally industrial). The principal working capital fund in the DON is NWCF.

2103. <u>CLASSIFICATION OF GOVERNMENT PROPERTY</u>. Government property includes all physical assets owned by the government. The classes of plant property (Marine Corps-owned real property and personal property of a capital nature) are:

1. <u>Class 1</u>. Land.

2. <u>Class 2</u>. Real property improvements to land, such as, buildings, structures, ground improvement structures, and utilities.

3. <u>General Personal Property, Plant and Equipment (PP&E)</u>. PP&E of a capital nature includes all assets:

    a. that have an estimated or actual initial acquisition cost that is equal to or greater than the DoD capitalization threshold as stated in FMR 7000.14-R, volume 4, chapter 6 (i.e., currently $100,000);

    b. that has an estimated recovery period equal to or greater than 24 months;

    c. that is not intended for sale in the ordinary course of operations;

    d. that has been acquired with the intention of being used, or available to be used by the DON in its operation; and

    e. these items are further defined as assets that are used to produce goods and/or services to support DON's mission, such as tangible equipment, industrial plant equipment, or other types of assets.

2104. CLASSIFICATION OF WORK. When a facility requirement is identified, the government property must first be categorized according to the classification of Government property as per the FMB Manual, volume 4, chapter 6. Second, the work associated with satisfying that requirement must be categorized according to the classification of work. Once the classification of work decision is made, the appropriate funding source for the requirement can then be determined. The classifications of work are:

1. Sustainment. Provides resources for maintenance and repair activities necessary to keep an inventory of facilities in good working order over a 50-year service life (see chapter 3).

2. Restoration and Modernization. Provides resources for improving facilities. Restoration includes repair and replacement work to restore facilities damaged by inadequate sustainment, excessive age, natural disasters, fire, accident, or other causes. Modernization includes construction or alterations of facilities solely to implement a new or higher standard, to accommodate new functions, or replace building components that typically last more than 50 years (see chapter 4).

3. Equipment Installation. Work to support the installation of personal property or collateral equipment in existing real property facility (see chapter 5).

2105. COMBINATION PROJECTS. Projects, which include a combination of construction, or repair, shall be separated and submitted as individual projects. The approval authority for each type of project shall apply. If a project that includes construction is so integrated as to preclude separation, the entire project shall be submitted as a construction project.

2106. SPECIAL CONSIDERATIONS

1. Phasing. Large sustainment projects may be phased to assure efficient use of available resources. Phasing of minor construction projects is strongly discouraged. Phasing may

permit accomplishment of the most urgent portion of a project within available funds, however funding limits will apply to the sum of all the phases.

2. Self-Help. DoD policy states that construction, repair, maintenance, and operation of real property must be accomplished through the most economic means available and be consistent with military and statutory requirements. To support the morale and retention of Marine Corps personnel, there is a continuing need to enhance the habitability of Bachelor Quarters and improve personnel support, welfare, and recreational facilities. A Self-Help Program can make such improvements using military personnel for maintenance, repair, alterations, and new construction. Additional guidance and responsibilities have been provided to all Marine Corps commands for the development and use of local Self-Help Programs (see MCO P11000.7).

2107. FACILITIES PROJECTS PROGRAM LIST. Special programs have been established to satisfy specific requirements.

1. Repair. Repair projects cover work to renew or replace deteriorated components of a facility, for its existing designated purpose. The projects are called M2 projects. These projects will be categorized as either sustainment or restoration and modernization.

2. Minor Construction. Minor construction projects cover work to build a new facility, or alter an existing facility that fall below the MILCON threshold. These projects are called R2. All minor construction projects fall under the restoration and modernization classification.

3. Minor Construction Special Programs. Listed below are the five special programs for minor construction work to satisfy specific requirements. Base personnel responsible for the functions (e.g., base safety manager for Occupational Safety and Health Act (OSHA) projects, etc.) must endorse by signature each DD Form 1391 submitted for consideration in these programs.

    a. Chapel Life Extension Program (CLEP).

    b. Physical Security Upgrade Program (PSUP).

    c. OSHA Program.

    d. Fire Protection Program (FIRE).

    e. Energy Investment Program (EIP).

Special program projects will be prioritized separately under their respective special program. Because these projects fall under CMC Special Program project funding, there is no minimum funding limit required to submit a project.

4. <u>Environmental Protection and Pollution Abatement Program</u>. Work classifications in this program include both environmental repair (ME) and environmental minor construction (ENV). The funding authority is the same as for regular M2/R2 projects (see appendix B). Installations will evaluate and classify each project as Environmental Quality Classes I, II, or III per MCO P5090.2. This classification will be annotated on the DD Form 1391 in block 10, Description of Proposed Work. Additionally, installations will submit with each project all environmentally related documentation required by MCO P5090.2.

5. <u>Demolition Program (DEMO)</u>. A portion of O&MMC major repair funds has been set aside to demolish excess or uneconomically reparable facilities. The CMC highly encourages the demolition of these structures in an effort to save utilities and maintenance costs. Installations shall submit projects during the annual CMC on-site project validation visit. This work should be classified as repair.

2108. <u>FRAUD, WASTE, AND ABUSE PREVENTION</u>

1. With the increase in volume of high dollar value projects, there must be an emphasis to prevent fraud, waste, and abuse (FWA). In the past, FWA has been largely attributed to an

agency's lack of internal controls. The Marine Corps' (FSRM) Facilities Sustainment, Restoration and Modernization programs must establish or strengthen controls to deal with potential FWA problems such as:

   a. Lacking of adequate and proper facilities maintenance resulting in untimely and costly repairs or replacements.

   b. Classifying construction as repair to use nonconstruction funds to do construction (R1/R2) projects.

   c. Incrementing construction to avoid MILCON planning and programming.

   d. "Goldplating" or procuring more goods and services than needed.

   e. Paying unreasonable prices for goods and services.

   f. Failing to consider life-cycle cost in planning and acquisition strategy.

2. The installation commander will insure the Facilities Projects Program complies with FWA requirements contained in MCO 7510.5 and MCO 5200.24. These directives provide policies and procedures to:

   a. Establish and maintain accounting and internal control systems over all funds, property, and other assets for which the command is responsible. This will ensure that:

      (1) Obligations and costs comply with all applicable laws.

      (2) All funds, property, and other assets are safeguarded against waste, loss, unauthorized use, or misappropriation.

        (3) Revenues and expenditures are recorded and properly
accounted.

    b.   Annually evaluate and report on the internal control
system per MCO 5200.24 as to their effectiveness and, if
applicable, to provide a plan of corrective action.

3.   The CMC reserves the right to conduct project reviews to
ensure compliance with the above requirement.

CHAPTER 2

PROCEDURES FOR FACILITIES PROJECTS

SECTION 2: PROJECT IDENTIFICATION AND DOCUMENTATION

2200. SCOPE. Project documentation is a critical first step
with three principle objectives. First, documentation provides
a methodology for addressing all factors related to the facility
requirement including operational, technical, financial, legal,
environmental, and social concerns. Second, it provides a
vehicle for obtaining, when required, approval and/or funding.
And third, documentation provides a record of what actions were
taken to address a particular facility requirement and how those
actions were funded. Procedures and provisions outlined in this
Manual cover all projects that fall within the CMC approval
limits specified in appendix B. Projects that fall within the
local commander's authority outlined in appendix B are exempt
from the provisions of this Manual.

2201. PROJECT IDENTIFICATION

1. Project Numbering. Each project must be assigned an
identification number. These identification numbers are
recorded on the project documentation. Approved projects will
carry the same project number through to completion of the
project. Non-approved projects should be assigned a new project
number when re-submitted for future consideration.

    a. Activity identification is accomplished by a two-
character alpha code shown in appendix C. These two alpha
characters are the first two letters in the project number.

    b. After the two-character alpha code, a four-digit numeric
series of project numbers is developed. The first two numbers
in the four-digit series denote the last two digits in the
fiscal year program for which the project submission is made.
The last two digits of the four-digit series are used to
sequentially number projects within each category of work.

c. When the total number of M2 or R2 projects proposed for the program exceeds 99, the four-digit numeric code in the project number will be increased to five numeric digits for those projects numbering above 99 only. For example, the project numbers assigned to projects following PE0299M will be PE02100M, PE02101M, PE02102M, etc.

d. After the four-digit numeric series, a single character alpha code will indicate the category of work as follows:

"M" for repair projects
"R" for minor construction projects

e. Environmental M2 and R2 projects will be identified by their COMPTrak number. All environmental projects must be entered into COMPTrak before they will be reviewed by CMC.

2. Project Titles. Project titles must specifically identify the facility function, building number, and the type of work to be done. Construction project titles shall include terms such as "addition", "extension", "alteration", and "expansion", as appropriate (e.g., "Expansion of Mess Hall, Building 43"). Repair project titles shall include the terms "repair" or "replace" as appropriate; less specific terms such as "rehabilitation" or "renovation" shall be avoided.

2202. DOCUMENTATION REQUIREMENTS. A list of required documentation for all projects presented for approval and execution in the HQMC Facilities Projects Program is listed on the K21 - Knowledge Management website at https://K21.hqmc.usmc.mil under Real Property Maintenance, Special Projects section. At a minimum, documentation should include the following:

1. A Completed DD Form 1391. Despite the title of the form, the "Military Construction Project Data", DD Form 1391 is the primary format to document O&MMC funded facilities projects. Appendix D contains samples of DD Form 1391, DD Form 1391c (the

continuation sheet). When construction projects are combined
with repair or equipment installation and the type of work is
separable, a separate DD Form 1391 shall be completed for each
type of work and cross-referenced. Each DD Form 1391 should
contain the following information:

a. Project Scope.

(1) The requirement associated with satisfying a
facility deficiency makes up the project scope. The project
scope must include all work necessary to produce a complete and
usable facility, or a complete and usable portion of a facility.

(2) Facility projects encompass a single real property
facility or utility. All work associated with meeting a
requirement in a particular facility must be incorporated in the
project scope. Where multiple projects are contemplated in a
single real property facility, see paragraphs 3303, and 4302.

(3) Properly identifying the project scope is
independent of the selected method(s) of accomplishing the work.
If the selected method of accomplishment is a construction
contract, then appropriate consideration should be given to the
proper scope of the contract. There is, however, no direct
relationship between contract scope and project scope.
Additional guidance on project scope can be found in paragraphs
2400.9, 3303, and 4302.

(4) Certain design criteria is triggered when a
restoration project exceeds a designated percentage of the PRV.
Project scopes that exceed 75 percent of the PRV of the facility
shall be programmed as MILCON.

(5) Restoration and Modernization projects on buildings
50 years or older require the net present value of repair not to
exceed 75% of the net present value of new construction.

b. Project Justification. Each project must be justified
on the basis of mission, life-cycle economics, health and
safety, environmental compliance, pollution prevention, quality
of life, or some combination of the above criteria. The need
for a proposed project must be supported by verifiable cost
data, and an adequate description of the requirement in the
narrative portions of the project documents.

c. Project Technical Solution. The proposed solution to a facilities requirement must withstand critical review by competent technical experts. Technical solutions should address concerns for reliability, maintainability, constructability, life cycle cost, sustainable design considerations, and safety. When applicable, technical solutions must also address concerns for legal compliance, energy conservation, environmental compliance, and the use of unproven technologies. In all cases, the benefits resulting from the technical solution must be weighed against the cost. Installations are responsible to ensure proper technical reviews are performed. CMC (LFF) may perform technical reviews. Bases will be notified if reviews are necessary.

d. Associated Unfunded Costs. The DD Form 1391 will clearly identify any associated unfunded costs that are required to make the facility complete and useable. These costs include, but are not limited to, collateral equipment, telecommunications cost, and audiovisual requirements. It is the installation's responsibility to ensure all funding requirements have been coordinated.

2. NAVFAC Form 11013/7. Cost Estimating Form, NAVFAC 11013/7, or a similar form shall be used in submitting cost estimates for all special projects. Cost estimates shall be sufficiently detailed to permit accurate determination of scope of work required, appropriate level of approval authority, and adequacy of requested funds. A lump sum allowance for contingency shall be included. Cost estimates shall be prepared in accordance with Appendix D.

3. Economic Analysis.

a. A formal net present value life-cycle economic analysis is required for:

(1) All repair projects with an estimated cost which is greater than $750,000 and more than 50 percent of the facility's PRV.

(2) All repair projects with an estimated per facility cost greater than $2 million.

b. Guidelines and formats for preparing economic analyses are contained in the NAVFAC P-442. Discount factors are update

annually and published in the Office of Management and Budget
(OMB) Note 7111. Results of analyses are to be submitted with
other required documentation.

   c. PRV times 1.25 (to allow for demolition and other
related costs) will be used as the replacement value of a
facility when developing an economic analysis.

4. Facility Planning Document (FPD). The FPD is the primary
tool for demonstrating continuing military need of the facility.
FPDs are required for all projects except where specifically
excluded by the NAVFAC P-72.

5. Site Location Maps. Site location maps, when appropriate,
should show pertinent physical features, such as distances from
the proposed improvement to existing structures, and utility
systems, proposed utility systems, and road extensions pertinent
to the project.

6. Site Approvals. Construction of new Class 2 facilities,
relocation of facilities at installations, and changes in the
basic function of a facility resulting in a change in the three-
digit category code require site approvals. Requests for Site
Approval (NAVMC 11069) will be completed as detailed in MCO
P11000.12.

7. National Environmental Policy Act (NEPA). Documentation of
all facilities projects covered in this manual, as defined in
paragraph 1002 will contain information required by the NEPA
regarding categorical exclusions, environmental assessments, or
environmental impact statements. The project documentation will
not be complete without this information, and the CMC
representative will not validate the project during the on-site
visit without a draft copy of this documentation at a minimum.

8. COMPTrak Project Detail Report (PDR). A PDR is required for
all environmental projects. Prepare and forward the PDR to the
CMC (LFL) for inclusion in the OMB, A-106 report. No
environmental project will be considered for approval unless
project documentation includes a copy of the current PDR.

9. Environmental Violations. Any environmental project which
corrects an EPA category class I deficiency must include a copy
of the noncompliance or enforcement letter, or a copy of the
notice or regulation which requires implementation of the

project prior to a specific deadline.

10. Additional Supporting Documentation. In addition to the
requirements listed above, projects should be supported with
studies, photographs, single line sketches, charts, maps, and
drawings to the extent necessary to fully communicate the
location, scope, complexity, unusual costs, and urgency of the
project. These documents, which supplement the narrative
description of the project, will often reduce review time and
expedite project approval and funding.

2203.   OTHER DOCUMENTATION REQUIREMENTS.

1. After the submission of the initial project documents,
installations will provide revised DD Form 1391 for each project
in which the project cost has changed by 20 percent or more
during design to reflect the updated cost of the final project
plans, specifications and engineering estimates. The revised DD
Form 1391 should be provided using the Project Update Request
function on the FI Website at https://www.hqmc-facilities.org.

2. The installation is responsible for ensuring all required
documentation is complete and accurate prior to requesting
authority to advertise. The installation shall retain a copy of
all required project documentation, correspondence, approvals,
and authorizations in their project files for at least three
years after the last contract action. Installations will have
documentation available for review upon request by CMC.

CHAPTER 2

PROCEDURES FOR FACILITIES PROJECTS

SECTION 3: PROJECT SUBMISSION

2300. <u>SUBMISSION PROCESS</u>. The Facilities Projects Program balances the Marine Corps decentralized operation and maintenance of physical plant assets with appropriate CMC oversight to ensure consistency and program integrity. Key steps in the process are discussed in the following paragraphs.

2301. <u>PLANNING AND PROGRAMMING</u>. Planning and programming are administrative steps that involve projecting requirements into the future and allocating resources to the highest priority needs. These actions are generally carried out at both the activity and the CMC levels. The purpose for these steps is to provide a mechanism for making investment decisions concerning real property assets.

2302. <u>PROJECT VALIDATION</u>

1. Projects above the installation commander's authority, as listed in appendix B, must receive approval by the CMC (LFF). The CMC conducts an annual on-site validation of these projects by sending a CMC representative to each activity during the 1st and 2d quarters of each fiscal year to survey projects proposed for execution. Prior to the validator coming on-site, each installation must enter all projects being presented for validation on the FI Website's New Project utility at https://www.hqmc-facilities.org. Each project will be surveyed using the CMC validation forms. The CMC representative will review and validate all projects that has a reasonable chance of being funded. The validation will include verification of:

    a. Proper classification of government property.

    b. Proper classification of work.

   c.   Proper source of funds.

   d.   Adequacy of the technical solution.

   e.   Completeness of scope and cost estimate.

   f.   Adequacy of economic analysis (when required).

   g.   Compliance with the Shore Facilities Planning System.

   h.   Compliance with environmental requirements per
MCO P5090.2A requirements, NEPA compliance, and safety
compliance.

   i.   Validation that the Commanding Officer's Readiness
Reporting System (CORRS) reflects a deficiency in this area.

2.   The installation commanders are responsible for the validity
and accuracy of facilities projects prepared for their plant nt,
including satisfying requirements for site approval such as
explosive or airfield safety (see MCO P11000.12) and earthquake
safety investigation (see NAVFACINST 11012.145).

3.   Validation Forms.   Current validation forms for major
repair, minor construction, and special program projects can be
obtained from the K21 Website at https://k21.hqmc.usmc.mil under
the Real Property Maintenance's Special Projects Section.
Installations will complete the heading of each validation form
for each project and provide the form to the CMC representative.

4.   Year of Execution.   Projects validated will normally be
planned for execution 2 years from the year of validation.
Under extenuating circumstances, the CMC representative will
validate supplemental projects for near term execution (see
paragraph 2303).   Projects will be numbered to reflect planned
year of execution.

5.   Approval of Special Program Projects.   The CMC
representative surveys special program projects concurrently
with major repair and regular minor construction projects (see

paragraph 2107). The respective special program manager at HQMC receives the surveyed projects from all the installations and compiles them into a single prioritized list. The validation score generated during the on-site validation is not necessarily the deciding factor in ranking a project on the list. Other factors, which the program manager deems relevant in prioritizing projects, are also applied and may override the validation score. Installations are notified of projects approved for design and funding during the current fiscal year by message. Projects not selected and authorized for design or funding in one fiscal year must be renumbered and resubmitted for consideration in future year programs.

6. Notification of Validation Results. Following the on-site validation, the CMC (LFF) will transmit, via the FI Website, a list of surveyed projects with their validation score.

7. Projects Requiring Additional Approvals. For projects requiring additional approvals, the CMC (LFF) will prepare an endorsement and forward the project to the appropriate approval authority. For projects requiring no further approvals, project approval shall be as designated by the CMC (LFF).

2303. SUPPLEMENTAL PROJECTS. Supplemental projects are those projects submitted either between annual on-site validation visits or for execution prior to the timeframe of the on-site validation visit.

1. A supplemental project shall be submitted only when at least one of the following criteria is satisfied:

    a. The project is urgently required to support a change in mission.

    b. Restoration is required immediately because of a natural disaster or similar act or circumstance beyond the control of the installation commander.

    c.   The project is self-amortizing within 3 years following
the completion of the project. Economic justification for such
projects shall be per NAVFAC P-422.

    d.   A hazard to life and property equating to the OSHA, Risk
Assessment Code (RAC) I, exists and cannot be corrected without
the requested project.

    e.   The project is urgently required due to an unforeseen
requirement or a change in environmental regulation/compliance
orders that jeopardizes continued use of the activity unless a
corrective project is initiated.

2.   The request for approval of a supplemental project shall
include all required documentation, a detailed explanation of
the circumstances generating the requirement, and the following
statement: "Project is submitted for approval as fiscal year
( ) supplemental project pursuant to MCO P11000.5( ), paragraph
2303.1( )". Insert appropriate fiscal year, the MCO's current
edition revision letter, and subparagraph number (a, b, c, d, or
e) in the parenthesis.

3.   Supplemental projects that meet the criteria outlined in
paragraph 2303.1b, d, or e shall be classified as restoration
and modernization projects (see chapter 5).

2304.   ASSISTANT SECRETARY OF NAVY (INSTALLATIONS AND
        ENVIRONMENT) (ASN (I&E)) APPROVAL

1.   In addition to the validation discussed in paragraph 2302,
repair projects over $5 million must receive an additional
approval by the ASN (I&E). These repair projects must be
consistent with force structure plans, be more cost effective
than replacement, and an appropriate use of O&M funds. Projects
in excess of $10 million require congressional notification in
addition to approval by ASN (I&E).

2.   Projects should be submitted as part of the validation
process. The CMC (LFF) will forward the project to the ASN
(I&E) and indicate in the endorsement the fiscal year (or years

in the case of phased projects) in which the project funding is planned. Notification of approval will be posted on the FI Website.

3. Once approved by the ASN (I&E) at a specific cost level, that amount may not be exceeded by more than 25 percent during execution without additional approval by ASN (I&E). Requests for approval of increased amounts should address the scope of the change, cost of the change, reason for cost increase, and a complete revised cost estimate. Local installations in coordination with the contracting office handling the construction contract must advise the CMC (LFF) of pending changes which will result in exceeding the prior approved amount.

CHAPTER 2

PROCEDURES FOR FACILITIES PROJECTS

SECTION 4: PROJECT EXECUTION

2400. <u>EXECUTION PROCESS</u>

1. <u>Execution Sequence</u>. After validation, execution of the
program follows these general steps:

    a. The CMC approves projects for design and provides A&E
funds. A&E funds are not provided for specific project and may
be used for any approved FSRM project.

    b. Installations advise the CMC of when designs will be
ready and priority of projects via semi-annual Contract
Advertisement Forecasts (CAF).

    c. Installations submit updated documentation, as required,
for changes in project scope or cost.

    d. The CMC (LFF) grants authority to advertise and commits
funds.

    e. Installations advise the CMC (LFF) of low bids and
request funds.

    f. The CMC allocates funds.

    g. Installations execute contract and obligate funds.

    h. Installation updates real property records to reflect
any change based on completed work.

2. <u>Project Design</u>. Normally, the CMC will preposition A&E
funds at the installations prior to the on-site validation
visit. After the Marine Corps-wide validation process, program
execution begins with notification from the CMC (LFF) of the

projects approved for A&E design. This notification will
normally be sent during third quarter of the fiscal year.
Installations may execute design contracts upon notification of
the projects approved for the program.

3. Project Plans and Specifications (PP&S) Review. Certain
approved projects will require the review of their PP&S by the
CMC. The determination of whether or not a project requires a
PP&S review is based upon the scope of work and other project
data provided on the DD Form 1391. The CMC (LFF) will notify
your installation which projects are required to undergo PP&S
review.

4. CAF. A forecast of when projects will be ready for contract
advertisement shall be provided by each activity semi-annually
by 15 March and 15 September of each year. The 15 March
submission will be used by the CMC to plan the straddle program
and 15 September submission will be used to develop the next
fiscal year program. Submission of the CAF will be via the CAF
module of the FI Website at https://www.hqmc-facilities.org. In
submitting the forecast, installations shall provide the most
current CWE, when the project is available for advertisement,
the relative priority of each project, and any associated
unfunded costs (see paragraph 2202.1d). Each program (M2, R2,
and individual special programs) shall be prioritized and listed
separately. If the project's current CWE is greater than 20
percent of the approved CWE in the FI website, a new DD Form
1391 will be required before the project can be listed on the
CAF. See paragraph 2203.1 for details.

5. Authority to Advertise. The CMC (LFF) will use the CAFs,
along with the installation's CORRS report, to determine which
projects will receive authority to advertise. The CMC (LFF)
will commit funds in the amount of the government estimate and
hold them in reserve at CMC. The committed amount (or maximum
amount established by the CMC) may not exceed 20 percent of the
original government estimate without additional approval from
the CMC (LFF). Requests for approval of increased amounts will
be submitted via the Project Update Module of the FI Website at

https://www.hqmc-facilities.org and include a revised DD Form 1391 detailing the new government estimate and addressing any change in scope. Additionally, a justification for the cost increase and a detailed cost estimate may be required on a project-by-project basis. If authorized projects are not advertised within the time period specified, the funds committed to the project may be withdrawn and the project canceled from the execution schedule.

6. Bid Opening Date (BOD). Installations will report BODs for all projects granted authority to advertise immediately upon such dates being established. Any change to a scheduled BOD should also be promptly reported. BODs can be updated using the BOD Update utility in the FI Website at https://www.hqmc-facilities.org.

7. Bid Opening and Request for Funds. Once the confirmed low bid has been determined, you may request funds for contract award using the Request for Funds module of the FI Website at https://www.hqmc-facilities.org.

8. Straddle Program. Projects authorized from the 15 March CAF shall have a scheduled bid opening from the last week of August through the second week of September and shall have at least a 60-day bid expiration period. These "straddle" bids provide the flexibility of using either current year or the following year funds. The number of projects approved for the "straddle" is determined by the amount of additional funds that are expected to be available and must be obligated before the year-end.

9. Contract Modifications

   a. There are three broad categories of contract modification:

      (1) Unforeseen Conditions. These modifications are beyond the A&E's ability to anticipate.

      (2) Design. These are changes that have resulted from poor design or lack of design. The A&E may be responsible for

some of the additional cost incurred. It is NAVFAC's responsibility to follow-up on design change orders and investigate A&E liability.

      (3) <u>Customer Requested</u>. These are changes that the activity requests to be made to the contract. Many times these changes could have been incorporated during the design effort and should have been competitively bid with the contract. The CMC highly discourages these and <u>will normally require the activity to fund this type of contract modification</u>.

    b. Concerted efforts shall be made to keep contract modifications to a minimum. Contract modification rates will be monitored by the activity, with records retained for review by CMC inspectors.

    c. When a contract modification is required and the total project costs are above the contingency ceiling that has been authorized, a request for an increase in the contingency ceiling limit must be submitted to the CMC (LFF) via the Contract Modification module in the FI Website at https://www.hqmc-facilities.org. The installation cannot proceed with the change order until the CMC (LFF) approves this request and a new contingency ceiling has been established.

    d. Contract modification funding is the responsibility of each installation. If the appropriate local funds are not available, and the modification must be accomplished, the installation should be prepared to reduce project scope in order to fund the required change. Installations may submit a contract modification funding request via the FI Website at https://www.hqmc-facilities.org but funding is not guaranteed. Intermediate Commands are responsible for funding modification requests within their ability before forwarding them for to the CMC for funding. The request will be reviewed by the appropriate Intermediate Command and will include the following information:

      (1) <u>Historical Data</u>. To include the original amount of the contract and year funded, the A&E amount and year funded and

the list of all change orders, if any, to include the amount and year funded and which command provided the funding.

      (2) <u>Current Data</u>. To include the title of the contract modification, the amount and year of funds, the circumstance and justification for the change order, impact if not provided and if A&E liability will be pursued.

      e. If the contract modification requires current year funds, the installation will identify compensatory M2/R2 projects from which funds will be taken to cover the cost of the modification in their requests.

      f. The availability of prior year funds is limited. The lack of prior year funds may require deducting work from existing contracts to make funds available for a specific requirement.

10. <u>Real Property Records</u>. Following the completion of any major renovation, new construction or conversion project, installations must update the internet Navy Facilities Assets Data Store (iNFADS) to accurately reflect the facility condition to include condition upgrades from substandard to adequate.

CHAPTER 3

SUSTAINMENT

SECTION 1: GENERAL INFORMATION

3100. <u>DEFINITION</u>. Sustainment provides resources for
maintenance and repair activities necessary to keep an inventory
of facilities in good working order over a 50-year service life.
It includes regularly scheduled adjustments and inspections,
preventive maintenance tasks, and emergency response and service
calls for minor repairs. It also includes major repairs or
replacement of facility components that are expected to occur
periodically throughout the facility life-cycle.

3101. <u>GENERAL POLICY FOR SUSTAINMENT</u>

1. The work includes regular roof replacement, refinishing wall
surfaces, repairing and replacing heating, ventilation and air-
conditioning (HVAC) systems, replacing tile and carpeting, and
similar type work. When sustainment involves replacement of
constituent parts, the items installed shall serve the same
purpose.

2. Sustainment does not include any construction. Sustainment
does not include repairing or replacing non-attached equipment
or furniture, or building components that typically last more
than 50 years (e.g., foundation and structural members).
Sustainment does not include repair work classified as
restoration or modernization (see chapter 4), environmental
compliance, or historical preservation. Other tasks associated
with facilities operations (such as custodial services, grass
cutting, landscaping, waste disposal, and the provision of
central utilities) are also not included.

3. Replacing landscaping destroyed by a sustainment project
shall be classified as sustainment.

CHAPTER 3

SUSTAINMENT

SECTION 2: MAINTENANCE

3200. DEFINITION. Maintenance is the recurring, day-to-day, periodic, or scheduled work required to preserve a real property facility to such a condition that it may be used for its designated purpose. The term includes work undertaken to prevent damage to a facility that otherwise would be more costly to repair.

3201. TYPE(S) OF MAINTENANCE

1. Specific maintenance is maintenance work on a facility performed on a specific job. This work is not of a continuing nature. Submission of maintenance work as a special project request shall be the exception rather than the rule. Only in highly unusual cases can a special project request for maintenance be submitted to the CMC (LFF) through the validation process. Maintenance work should only be submitted for funding as a special project when the work is beyond the local resources normally provided and the work is better accomplished as a single undertaking and must be accomplished on time. These cases include:

   a. Dredging to a previously established depth.

   b. Major seal-coating of asphalt pavement.

   c. Resealing all joints in runway concrete pavement.

   d. Major waterproofing and painting to preserve exterior and interior walls of buildings.

2. Recurring maintenance is preventive or recurring work to maintain the facility in operable condition. This work is highly repetitive on a portion of a facility. Recurring maintenance shall be programmed in an installation's budget.

3202. <u>APPROVAL AUTHORITY</u>. The maximum specific approval
authorities for all activities are listed in appendix B. This
authority may be reduced by the CMC.

CHAPTER 3

SUSTAINMENT

SECTION 3: REPAIR

3300. <u>DEFINITION</u>. Repair is to return a real property facility, system, or component to such a condition that it may effectively be used for its designated functional purpose.

1. Repairs to an existing facility may include modification or addition of building or facility components or materials which are required for compliance with current life safety standards, recognized national or regional building codes, or environmental regulations. Items that may be classified repair under these guidelines include:

    a. Correcting seismic or life safety deficiencies.

    b. Installing fire protection.

    c. Removal of asbestos material.

    d. Antiterrorism/Force Protection requirements.

2. Repair is classified as sustainment except when it meets one of the four criteria outlined in paragraph 4202. Then it will be classified as restoration and modernization.

3. Consistent with the definition of construction, repair does not include additions, expansions, alterations, or modifications required solely for a change in purpose or mission, or in preparation for future construction requirements.

3301. <u>GENERAL POLICY FOR REPAIR PROJECTS</u>

1. When repair projects involve replacement of constituent parts, the items installed shall serve the same purpose.

2. Repairs may include replacement of the current materials with substitute materials.

3. Incident to a major facility repair the following work may be classified within the scope of repair:

    a. Relocation and minor additions to components in an existing facility to return it to its customary state of operating efficiency, to allow for effective use of existing space, or to meet current building code requirements (e.g., additional partitions installed during repair of deteriorated interior partitions).

    b. Replacement of deteriorated facility components, built-in equipment, or systems with items of higher quality, more durable materials or greater capacity to conform with current design criteria or meet increased demands/standards. The replacement items will not change the function of the components, equipment, or systems, unless there is no alternative to such replacements.

4. Energy efficient maintenance permits the repair by replacement of fully functioning energy consuming equipment or systems with more efficient equipment when:

    a. The cost of replacing the energy consuming equipment or system can be recovered through cost savings within 10 years,

    b. The replacement does not substantially increase the capacity of the equipment or systems, and

    c. The new equipment or system provides the same end product (e.g., cooling, heat, and lighting), even though the equipment is not replaced in kind. For example, a leaking steam line serving a small, remote load may be "repaired" at the lowest life-cycle cost by installing a local boiler or heat pump at the load and by decommissioning the steam line. Repair projects for energy efficient maintenance must include all work necessary to make the new, more efficient equipment or system complete and operational.

5. The following actions shall not be classified as repair:

    a. Extension of facility systems or components to areas not being repaired or previously served (e.g., extension of air conditioning system to a floor or wing not previously cooled).

    b. Increases to exterior facility dimensions or utility plant capacity, except as required for handicapped access or fire egress.

    c. Alterations to existing bachelor quarters solely intended to meet current DoD or Marine Corps design standards.

6. Demolition.

    a. Demolition of a facility or a portion of a facility is classified as repair when the extent of deterioration is such that it can no longer be economically be maintained or when the facility is a hazard to the health and safety of personnel.

    b. In order to ensure compliance with McKinney Act requirements, approval of the cognizant COMNAVFACENGCOM Engineering Field Division (EFD) is required prior to demolition of any facilities that are not being replaced. For demolition projects that affect properties of historic or cultural significance, see MCO P5090.2.

7. For facilities project purposes, a utility system is a single real property facility that may include generation plant equipment, distribution lines and associated distribution equipment, and the building(s) or structure(s) that house these equipment components. Buildings, which house utility systems or their components, if properly justified, are considered components of the utility system real property facility.

8. In the case that a barracks is taken off line for a major repair the following will occur:

    a. The installation of a fire sprinkler system will be part of the repair for those barracks rooms lacking such a system.

    b. Cost for the installation of a fire sprinkler system will be contracted as a separate bid item. (additive)

c. If there is any reason the installation of a fire sprinkler system should not occur during a major repair then the installation must submit a request to HQMC. The approval/disapproval authority is held by HQMC.

3302. <u>FUNDING OF REPAIR</u>. Repair projects shall be funded from appropriations available for O&MMC or from internally generated funds at NWCF activities. Repair of facilities, which suffer extensive damage from natural disasters, may be accomplished and funded from supplemental appropriations for MILCON (see MCO P11000.12).

3303. <u>SCOPE OF REPAIR PROJECTS</u>.

1. A project is defined as a single undertaking necessary to satisfy a finite work requirement. A "finite requirement" of repair is considered to be all the work necessary to maintain serviceability or to prevent significant deterioration of a real property facility or a component of the facility. Normally, all planned major repairs in a single facility will be included in a single project. Multiple projects, however, may be undertaken for independent repair requirements. Each phase must result in a complete and usable facility.

2. Deficiencies in an individual facility are normally detected as a part of the control inspection or specialized inspection programs (see MCO P11000.7). When prudent management dictates that such work of special project scope be scheduled and accomplished with local funds, it may be accomplished with the approval of the CMC (LFF). Requirements for documentation and technical validation still apply. Real property facilities that are not required to satisfy the approved Facilities Requirements Plan should not be programmed for repair.

3304. <u>INCREMENTATION OF REPAIR</u>.

1. The scope of a repair project, or phase of a repair project, should result in a complete and usable facility or a complete and usable component of an existing facility.

2. Repairs shall not be subdivided into multiple projects for the purpose of avoiding approval by higher authority.

3. Repair projects that are phased shall be reviewed and approved based on the total cost of all phases.

3305. <u>APPROVAL AUTHORITY</u>. The maximum approval authorities for all activities are listed in appendix B. This authority may be reduced by the CMC.

CHAPTER 4

RESTORATION AND MODERNIZATION

SECTION 1: GENERAL INFORMATION

4100. DEFINITION. Restoration and Modernization provides resources for improving facilities. Restoration includes repair and replacement work to restore facilities damaged by inadequate sustainment, excessive age, natural disasters, fire, accident, or other cases. Modernization includes construction or alteration of facilities solely to implement a new or higher standard (including regulatory changes), to accommodate new functions, or replace building components that typically last more than 50 years (e.g., foundations and structural members).

4101. GENERAL POLICY FOR RESTORATION AND MODERNIZATION

1. Restoration and modernization does not include recurring sustainment tasks or certain environmental measures that are funded elsewhere.

2. Other tasks associated with facilities operations (such as custodial services, grass cutting, landscaping, waste disposal, and the provision of central utilities) are also not included.

CHAPTER 4

RESTORATION AND MODERNIZATION

SECTION 2: REPAIR

4201. DEFINITION. Repair returns a real property facility, system or component from a seriously degraded state to its original unimpaired form, or to an improved condition incorporating current recognized standards such that it may effectively be used for its designated functional purpose are classified as restoration and modernization.

4202. RESTORATION AND MODERNIZATION CRITERIA FOR REPAIR PROJECTS.

1. Repair projects that contain the following types of work, and the value of work exceeds 50 percent of project cost, are classified as restoration and modernization.

    a. The purpose of the repair project is to restore additional damage caused by lack of sustainment.

    b. The repair project is for the sole purpose of implementing a regulatory requirement. This includes environmental regulation/compliance orders, seismic repairs, life safety requirements (RAC I) and antiterrorism/force protection upgrades.

    c. The repair project is required for the restoration of a real property facility because of a natural disaster or an accident.

    d. The repair project involves replacing the foundation or structural members of a real property facility.

2. Repair projects whose scope exceeds 75 percent of the PRV of the facility shall be programmed as MILCON.

3.   Repair projects on buildings over 50 years old must show a net present value analysis if the net present value of repair is less than 75 percent of the net present value of new construction.

CHAPTER 4

RESTORATION AND MODERNIZATION

SECTION 3: CONSTRUCTION

4300. DEFINITIONS.

1. Construction. Construction is the erection, installation, or assembly of a new real property facility; or the addition, expansion, extension, alteration, conversion, or replacement of an existing real property facility; or the relocation of a real property facility. Construction projects include the demolition of facilities (unless demolition can be categorized as repair IAW paragraph 3301.6), supporting utilities, roads, parking lots, equipment installed in and made a part of such facilities, related site preparation, excavation, filling and landscaping, or other land improvements incident to the project.

2. Conversion. A conversion to a real property facility contains two necessary elements: (a) a major structural revision, and (b) a change in functional purpose resulting in a change to the facility's current 3-digit basic category code (NAVFAC P-72). When a conversion project also includes repairs and/or maintenance, the separate categories of work will be funded as such.

3. Addition, Expansion, Extension. Addition, expansion, and extension each constitute a physical increase to a real property facility. As a general rule, if the dimensions used to record the facility in the inventory are increased, then an addition, expansion, or extension has occurred. Modernization that increases production capability, enlarges, extends, or expands primary distribution systems, or provides services for a new purpose is construction.

4. Replacement. A replacement is a complete reconstruction of a real property facility destroyed or damaged beyond economical repair. Replacement or a major reconstruction, such as the

removal of a deteriorated building and erection of a new building on an existing foundation, are construction and not repair, except for utility plant buildings that are part of the utility system (see paragraph 3301.7). There is no such thing as repair by replacement for a complete facility. A construction project for complete replacement must include the cost of demolition of the replaced facility.

5. Alteration. An alteration is the work required in adjusting interior arrangements or other physical characteristics (not in a deteriorated state) of an existing facility so that it may be more effectively adapted to or used for its designated purpose. Alteration is classified as construction. Minor alteration incidental to a major repair of a facility can be classified as repair.

4301. TYPES OF CONSTRUCTION

1. Minor Construction

   a. A minor construction project is a single undertaking with a funded cost of $750,000 or less (including contract administration or SIOH). The project shall include all work necessary to produce a complete and usable facility or a complete and usable improvement to an existing facility. All minor construction projects for an addition, expansion, extension or alteration must be supported by the Facilities Planning and Programming System (see MCO P11000.12).

   b. In instances where the project is intended solely to correct a deficiency that is life threatening, health threatening, or safety threatening, the minor construction funding threshold is $1.5 million (including contract administration or SIOH). Life and safety threatening is defined as a hazard to human life, equating to the OSHA Risk Assessment Code (RAC) I or II. Health threatening is defined as a severe health situation existing in the near or long term. These situations can include, but are not limited to, projects to correct conditions that contribute to environmental contamination.

2. <u>MILCON</u>. A MILCON project is defined as a single undertaking with a funding cost in excess of $750,000 that includes all construction necessary to produce a complete and usable facility, or a complete and usable improvement to an existing facility. MILCON projects must received congressional approval in both authorization and appropriations laws before construction can begin.

3. <u>Unspecified Minor Construction (UMC)</u>. An UMC project is defined as a single undertaking with a funded cost in excess of $750,000 that includes all urgent construction necessary to produce a complete and usable facility or a complete and usable improvement to an existing facility. The maximum amount specified by law for an unspecified minor MILCON project is currently $1,500,000, and such projects are funded from the MILCON appropriations.

4302. <u>CONSTRUCTION INCREMENTATION</u>

1. No project may be subdivided for reasons of circumventing programming and approval requirements. Each project must result in a complete and usable real property facility, or complete and usable improvement to an existing facility. The planned (foreseeable) acquisition of, or improvement to, a real property facility through a series of minor construction projects is prohibited. Minor construction work which will involve multiple facilities required by a new mission, must be treated as follows:

    a. Where the multiple facilities involved are all the same category code, the work must be incorporated into a single scope, if it is required to implement a specific mission change. For example, if 24 magazines at an installation must undergo alterations in connection with a new ordnance-handling mission, this work would be accomplished as a single project. If the work is not required by the new mission, then each construction decision is independent.

b.   Where the multiple facilities involved are different category codes, the work will generally be incorporated into a single scope, unless it can be demonstrated that the work in each facility:

     (1) Is for unrelated and dissimilar purposes,

     (2) Is not dependent on each other, and

     (3) Will result in each being a complete and usable facility or a complete and usable improvement to a facility.

A new mission is defined as a requirement, not previously required or performed, imposed on the Marine Corps by the CMC, DoD, Congress, or the President.

2.   The following actions are prohibited:

     a.   Splitting a project scope solely to avoid an approval requirement, or to circumvent the statutory limitation on funding minor construction with an appropriation other than MILCON.

     b.   Splitting a requirement when it may result in a higher cost of construction because of the sacrifice of economy of scale. For example, construction of multiple small buildings, each under $750,000, instead of a single, more economical building.

     c.   Working concurrently on an active military construction project to avoid MILCON reprogramming approval procedures.

3.   A complete and usable facility may require extensions or improvements to other supporting facilities, such as exterior electrical, water, and sewage distribution systems, parking lots, and fencing. Exterior utility modifications must be included in the construction project scope, except in cases where central utility modifications are required to support several new facilities or upgrades in more than one facility.

4303. COMBINING APPROPRIATED AND PRIVATE OR NON-APPROPRIATED
       FUNDS

1. Appropriated funds should not be combined with private or
non-appropriated funds for the same minor construction project.
This practice may be considered incrementation and subdivision
to circumvent statutory limitations. Exceptions to this policy
must be approved in advance by the Secretary of the Navy or the
appropriate designee. Requests for exceptions to this policy
shall be submitted to the CMC (LFF) for submission to the ASN
(I&E) for approval.

2. Private or non-appropriated funds may be used to purchase
and install furnishings, equipment, and interior finishes for
private and non-appropriated fund facilities. Mixing of
appropriated and private or non-appropriated funds for repair or
maintenance projects is allowed.

3. Appropriated funds, normally not allowed for construction of
revenue generating facilities, may be used only in those
instances authorized by the funding policy outlined in FMB
Manual, volume 7, chapter 5, paragraphs 075530 and 075531.
Request for approval should be submitted to the CMC (LFF), for
submission to ASN (I&E) (see SECNAVINST 7000.23).

4304. MULTIPLE MINOR CONSTRUCTION PROJECTS IN THE SAME REAL
PROPERTY FACILITY. Multiple minor construction projects in an
existing single facility may be allowed when they are: (1) for
unrelated and dissimilar purposes, (2) not dependent on each
other, (3) not contiguous (not touching), and (4) each one will
result in a complete and usable improvement to the facility.

4305. CONSTRUCTION IN GENERAL SERVICES ADMINISTRATION-OWNED,
MANAGED OR CONTROLLED FACILITIES. Under the general provisions
in the annual appropriations for the General Services
Administration (GSA), Marine Corps appropriations available for
operations and maintenance may be used for reimbursement to the
GSA for the expenses of renovation and alteration of buildings

and facilities. Therefore, projects involving alterations to Marine Corps-occupied, GSA-owned, managed, or controlled facilities shall be authorized and funded by the CMC or the Marine Corps activity requiring the work. The GSA is responsible for work that a tenant can normally expect from a landlord. The Marine Corps is responsible for work which cannot be normally expected from a landlord and which is strictly peculiar to the needs of the Marine Corps. When Marine Corps appropriations are used to fund construction (including alterations) or repair of GSA-owned, managed, or controlled facilities, the provisions of this Manual apply. O&M funds shall not be used for work in GSA-owned, managed, or controlled facilities that would otherwise require MILCON appropriation funding. For the purposes of these provisions, industrial funds are considered similar to appropriations available for O&M. The above policy is also applicable to non-GSA administered facilities leased by the Marine Corps that are subject to the provisions of NAVFAC P-73, "Real Estate Procedural Manual."

4306. <u>FUNDING OF MINOR CONSTRUCTION</u>. Construction programming authority described below is only applicable to minor construction. Refer to MCO P11000.12 for details on all other construction programming. Minor construction projects shall be funded from appropriations available for O&MMC or from internally generated funds at NWCF activities.

4307. <u>APPROVAL AUTHORITY</u>. The maximum approval authorities for all installations are listed in appendix B. This authority may be reduced by the CMC.

REAL PROPERTY FACILITIES MANUAL

CHAPTER 5

EQUIPMENT INSTALLATION

CHAPTER 5

EQUIPMENT INSTALLATION

SECTION 1: GENERAL INFORMATION

5100. DEFINITIONS. There are two categories of equipment related to Facilities Sustainment, Restoration, and Modernization:

1. Built-In Equipment. Built-in equipment is accessory equipment and furnishings that are not intended to be movable, are required for operation, and are permanently affixed as a part of the real property facility. The equipment is engineered and built into the facility as an integral part of the final design. Equipment of this nature is considered part of the class 2 real property facility, and is funded as construction. Examples of built-in equipment are:

   a. Built-in furniture, cabinets, and shelving.

   b. Venetian blinds and shades.

   c. Window screens and screen doors.

   d. Elevators and escalators.

   e. Fire alarms and protection systems (built-in).

   f. Heating, ventilating, and air-conditioning installations (except when provided solely to support a piece of collateral equipment).

   g. Electric generators and auxiliary gear, including uninterruptible power supply, in support of a real property facility electrical system.

   h. Hoods and vents.

    i. Non-movable cranes, hoists, and built-in rails for movable cranes.

    j. Chapel pews, pulpits, and theater seats.

2. <u>Collateral Equipment</u>. Collateral equipment covers all items, including furniture and furnishings, which are loose, portable, or can be easily detached from the structure and permanently attached equipment such as technical, medical, scientific, production, and processing equipment that is procured as collateral equipment. Examples of collateral equipment include:

    a. Loose furniture (including furniture bolted to the wall).

    b. Loose furnishings, including rugs.

    c. Filing cabinets and portable safes.

    d. Portable office machines.

    e. Messhall equipment.

    f. Training aids, equipment, and simulators.

    g. Shop equipment.

    h. Automated data processing equipment.

    i. Intrusion detection systems.

    j. Electric generators and UPS in support of collateral equipment.

    k. Window air-conditioning units.

    l. Portable cranes and hoists.

    m. Audiovisual equipment.

n. Automated Storage and Retrieval Systems.

o. Any operational equipment for which installation mounting and connections are provided in the building design and which are detachable without damage to the building or equipment (e.g., dynamometers).

5101. <u>INSTALLATION OF EQUIPMENT</u>. Equipment installation is a modification to real property required solely for the installation of an item of collateral equipment.

1. <u>Installation of Collateral Equipment in New Real Property Facilities</u>. In the construction of new facilities, the construction shall be complete and the facility ready to receive the collateral equipment. All known utilities, false floors, foundations, partitions, shielding, air-conditioning, ventilation, and other requirements incidental to the installation of the equipment that are integral to the facility shall be included in the construction cost and funded with the same appropriation used to construct the new facility. <u>The cost of making the final connections of the collateral equipment shall be funded from the same procurement appropriation used to fund the equipment purchase.</u>

2. <u>Installation of Collateral Equipment in Existing Real Property Facilities</u>. The cost of installing collateral equipment in existing facilities is funded from the same appropriation used to purchase the equipment. The equipment installation cost shall include all items in support of the equipment (false floors, shielding, concrete pads, secondary utilities, etc.), and the material and labor costs to install any ancillary equipment (air-conditioning, uninterruptible power supply, etc.). Other costs should be categorized as follows:

a. Costs for major structural changes to an existing facility, extension of its primary utility distribution system, or construction of a major exterior support structure required for the collateral equipment are construction costs.

    b.   The cost of relocating an item of collateral equipment from one location to an existing or new facility is funded by activity operating funds other than the FSRM account in the O&MMC appropriation.

CHAPTER 5

EQUIPMENT INSTALLATION

SECTION 2:   EQUIPMENT INSTALLATION PROGRAMMING

5200.   <u>APPROVAL AUTHORITY</u>.   Equipment installation in existing real property facilities is not a FSRM cost.   The command or agency that procures the equipment for the installation normally funds the cost of equipment installation.   Associated minor construction projects will compete equally for funding within the CMC projects program.

5201.   <u>SUBMISSION REQUIREMENTS</u>.   The procedures for submission of minor construction projects in support of equipment installation are contained in chapter 2.   The activity is responsible for coordinating the equipment installation through the command or agency that procures the equipment for installation.

CHAPTER 5

EQUIPMENT INSTALLATION

SECTION 3: TELECOMMUNICATIONS EQUIPMENT

5300. DEFINITION. Telecommunications equipment are devices and systems (e.g., telephone and automated data processing equipment, such as computers and computer networks) that allow for communications at a distance.

5301. TELECOMMUNICATIONS EQUIPMENT

1. Procurement, installation, repair, and replacement of telecommunication equipment is funded by appropriations other than O&MMC FSRM (e.g., telephone instruments, switchgear, desktop personal computers, etc.).

2. Installation of Telecommunications Equipment in New Real Property Facilities. Costs to install conduits, ducts, cabling, wiring, raceways, and support structures that are integral to the facility shall be included in the construction cost and funded with the same appropriation used to construct the facility. The wiring for voice and data telecommunications services shall comply with published Marine Corps standards.

3. Installation of Telecommunications Equipment in Existing Real Property Facilities. Costs to repair or install conduits, ducts, raceways, and support structures that are integral to the facility may be funded as a FSRM cost. Wiring and cabling must be funded by appropriations other than O&MMC FSRM if being replaced in kind; or with O&MMC FSRM minor construction funds if being installed or upgraded (NAVSO P1000.3M, paragraph 036107.b (1)).

4. The cost of final installation of the telecommunications equipment shall be funded from the same appropriation used to fund the telecommunications equipment purchase. The cost of

making final connections of relocated telecommunications
equipment shall be funded from O&MMC accounts other than FSRM.

5. Day-to-day telecommunications equipment replacements, minor
equipment rearrangements, and installations within the purview
of the installation commander, which do not require approval of
higher authority, are funded from local O&MMC accounts other
than FSRM.

5302. EXTERIOR TELECOMMUNICATIONS REQUIREMENTS

1. The acquisition and installation of Marine Corps-owned
telecommunications lines (cable, ducts, poles, manholes, etc.),
exterior to buildings is considered a utility system and shall
be classified a construction cost and funded with MILCON or
O&MMC FSRM funds. The cost of installing common ducts, poles,
manholes, etc., for telecommunications and electrical
distribution lines will also be funded as construction from
either MILCON or O&MMC FSRM accounts. The wiring for voice and
data telecommunications services shall comply with published
Marine Corps standards.

2. The repair of Marine Corps-owned telecommunications lines
exterior to a building is funded from O&MMC FSRM accounts.

3. Telecommunications carrier equipment (e.g., pulse code
modulation systems) installed to increase the distribution
system circuit to provide service to a new facility shall be
included as a funded project cost for the new facility using the
same appropriation to construct the new facility.

4. Telecommunications carrier equipment installed to upgrade
and serve existing systems and facilities shall be procured and
installed as personal property.

5. Funding for the procurement and installation of exterior
telecommunications cable not owned by the Marine Corps will be
from appropriations other than O&MMC FSRM.

APPENDIX A

ABBREVIATIONS/ACRONYMS

A&E	ARCHITECTURAL AND ENGINEERING
ASN	ASSISTANT SECRETARY OF THE NAVY
ATFP	ANTITERRORISM/FORCE PROTECTION
BOD	BID OPENING DATE
CAF	CONTRACT ADVERTISEMENT FORECAST
CLEP	CHAPEL LIFE EXTENSION PROGRAM
CMC	COMMANDANT OF THE MARINE CORPS
COMMARCORLOGCOM	COMMANDER, MARINE CORPS LOGISTICS COMMAND
COMNAVFACENGCOM	COMMANDER, NAVAL FACILITIES ENGINEERING COMMAND
COMMARFORLANT	COMMANDER, MARINE FORCES ATLANTIC
COMMARFORPAC	COMMANDER, MARINE FORCES PACIFIC
CO	COMMANDING OFFICER
CORRS	COMMANDING OFFICER'S READINESS REPORTING SYSTEM
COMPTRAK	COMPLIANCE TRACKING SYSTEM
CWE	CURRENT WORKING ESTIMATE
DEMO	DEMOLITION PROGRAM
DOD	DEPARTMENT OF DEFENSE
DON	DEPARTMENT OF THE NAVY
EFA	ENGINEERING FIELD ACTIVITY
EFD	ENGINEERING FIELD DIVISION
EIP	ENERGY INVESTMENT PROGRAM

ENV	ENVIRONMENTAL MINOR CONSTRUCTION PROGRAM
EPA	ENVIRONMENTAL PROTECTION AGENCY
ERN	ENVIRONMENTAL RESTORATION, NAVY
FI	FACILITIES INTEGRATION
FIRE	FIRE PROTECTION MINOR CONSTRUCTION PROGRAM
FPD	FACILITY PLANNING DOCUMENT
FSRM	FACILITIES SUSTAINMENT, RESTORATION AND MODERNIZATION
FWA	FRAUD, WASTE AND ABUSE
GSA	GENERAL SERVICES ADMINISTRATION
HQMC	HEADQUARTERS MARINE CORPS
HVAC	HEATING, VENTILATION AND AIR CONDITIONING
I&E	INSTALLATIONS AND ENVIRONMENT
INFADS	INTERNET NAVAL FACILITIES ASSETS DATA STORE
K21	KNOWLEDGE FOR THE 21ST CENTURY
MARFORRES	MARINE FORCES RESERVES
MILCON	MILITARY CONSTRUCTION
MAGTFTC	MARINE AIR GROUND TASK FORCE TRAINING COMMAND
MCAF	MARINE CORPS AIR FACILITY
MCAS	MARINE CORPS AIR STATION
MCB	MARINE CORPS BASE
MCCS	MARINE CORPS COMMUNITY SERVICES
MCLB	MARINE CORPS LOGISTICS BASE
MCRD	MARINE CORPS RECRUIT DEPOT

REAL PROPERTY FACILITIES MANUAL

ME	ENVIRONMENTAL REPAIR PROGRAM
NAF	NON-APPROPRIATED FUNDS
NAVFAC	NAVAL FACILITIES ENGINEERING COMMAND
NEPA	NATIONAL ENVIRONMENTAL POLICY ACT
NWCF	NAVY WORKING CAPITAL FUND
OMB	OFFICE OF MANAGEMENT AND BUDGET
O&M,MC	OPERATIONS AND MAINTENANCE, MARINE CORPS
OSHA	OCCUPATIONAL SAFETY AND HEALTH ADMINSTRATION
PDR	PROJECT DETAIL REPORT
PP&S	PROJECTS PLANS AND SPECIFICATION
PRV	PLANT REPLACEMENT VALUE
PSUP	PHYSICAL SECURITY UPGRADE PROGRAM
RDT&E	RESEARCH, DEVELOPMENT, TESTING AND EVALUATION
SIOH	SUPERVISION, INSPECTION, AND OVERHEAD
UPS	UNINTERRUPTIBLE POWER SUPPLY

REAL PROPERTY FACILITIES MANUAL

APPENDIX B

APPROVAL LEVELS

Major Activities

Category of Work	Cost Limits	Approval Request To	Approval Authority
1. Maintenance (M1)			
(a) Recurring (M1)	None	None	C.O.
(b) Specific (M1)	None	None	C.O.
2. Repair (M1/M2)	$0 - $300,000 (M1)	None	C.O.
	$300,001 - $5M (M2)	CMC (LFF)	CMC (LFF)
	Over $5 Million	CMC (LFF)	ASN (I&E)
	Over $7.5 Million	CMC (LFF)	Congress
3. Construction (R1/R2/MCON) (a) General	$0 - $100K (R1)	None	C.O.
	$100,001 - $750K (R2)	CMC (LFF)	CMC (LFF)
	Over $750K (MCON)	CMC (LFL)	Congress
(b) Solely to correct a life-, health-, or safety-threatening deficiency.	$750K to $1.5M (footnote 1)	CMC (LFF)	Congress

Minor Activities

Category of Work	Cost Limits	Approval Request To	Approval Authority
1. Maintenance (M1)			
(a) Recurring (M1)	None	None	C.O.
(b) Specific (M1)	None	None	C.O.
2. Repair (M1/M2)	$0 - $25,000 (M1)	None	C.O.
	$25,001 to $5M (M2)	CMC (LFF)	CMC (LFF)
	Over $5 Million	CMC (LFF)	ASN (I&E)
	Over $7.5 Million	CMC (LFF)	Congress
3. Construction (R1/R2) (a) General	$0 - $10,000 (R1)	None	C.O.
	$10,001 to $750K (R2)	CMC (LFF)	CMC (LFF)
	Over $750K (MCON)	CMC (LFL)	Congress
(b) Solely to correct a life-, health-, or safety-threatening deficiency.	$750K to $1.5M (footnote 1)	CMC (LFF)	Congress

Footnotes: (1) See paragraph 4301.1(b).

REAL PROPERTY FACILITIES MANUAL

APPENDIX C

LISTING OF ACTIVITY ALPHA CODES

ALPHA
CODE   ACTIVITY

AL   MCLB Albany, Georgia
BA   MCLB Barstow, California
BE   MCAS Beaufort, South Carolina
BP   MWTC Bridgeport, California
BU   MCB Camp Butler, Okinawa, Japan
CP   MCAS Cherry Point, North Carolina
EI   MARBKS, 8th & I, Washington, District of Columbia
EL   Camp Allen, Norfolk, Virginia
FD   First Marine Corps District, Garden City, New York
FU   MCAS Futenma, Okinawa, Japan
HH   HQBN HQMC Henderson Hall, Arlington, Virginia
HI   MCB Hawaii, Kaneohe Bay, Hawaii
IW   MCAS Iwakuni, Yamaguchi, Japan
KC   MCSA Kansas City, Missouri
LE   MCB Camp Lejeune, North Carolina
MI   MCAS Miramar, California
NR   MCAS New River, North Carolina
PA   MCAS Camp Pendleton, California
PE   MCB Camp Pendleton, California
PI   MCRD ERR Parris Island, South Carolina
QA   MCAF Quantico, Virginia
QU   MCB Quantico, Virginia
SD   MCRD WRR San Diego, California
TP   MAGTFTC Twentynine Palms, California
YU   MCAS Yuma, Arizona

REAL PROPERTY FACILITIES MANUAL

APPENDIX D

DD FORM 1391 AND INSTRUCTIONS

SAMPLE   DD Form 1391   **SAMPLE**

1. COMPONENT USMC	FY 2002 MILITARY CONSTRUCTION PROJECT DATA	2. DATE 05/15/00
3. INSTALLATION AND LOCATION MARINE CORPS BASE INSTALLATION A	4. PROJECT TITLE REPAIR WHARF 1312	

5. PROGRAM ELEMENT O&M,MC	6. FAC CODE 1520	7. PROJECT NUMBER IN0215M	8. PROJECT COST ($000) $2,860

9. COST ESTIMATES				
ITEM	U/M	QUANTITY	UNIT COST	COST ($000)
REPAIR/CONSTRUCT WHARF.........................	LF	1,060	2,000	2,120
Structure.....................................	LF	1,060	1,794.81	(1,903)
Excavation....................................	CY	5,000	43.50	(217)
SUPPORTING FACILITIES	LS	--	--	740
Utilities......................................	LS	--	--	(145)
Paving, Site Improvement and Demolition......	LS	--	--	(595)
SUBTOTAL (PROJECT COST)	--	--	--	2,860
CONTINGENCY (included)	--	--	--	--
CONTRACT ADMINISTRATION (8%)	--	--	--	229
TOTAL FUNDED COST	--	--	--	3,089
	--	--	--	
PLANNING AND DESIGN COST (__%)	--	--	--	309
	--	--	--	
EQUIPMENT FROM OTHER APPROPRIATIONS	--	--	--	(0)
	--	--	--	
	--	--	NON-ADD	

10. DESCRIPTION OF PROPOSED CONSTRUCTION

    The repairs are required to correct deterioration due to age and exposure to saltwater. The steel sheet pile bulkhead is severely corroded and rusted through. Fill material behind the bulkhead has filtered through the holes causing subsidence of the pavement surface. The project proposes installation of a new sheet pile bulkhead (capped with concrete) outboard of the existing bulkhead and filling the space between with new fill material

11. REQUIREMENT: 1,945 LF   ADEQUATE: 885 LF   SUBSTANDARD: 980 LF

   PROJECT

   The project will repair/replace the bulkhead and pavement ....

   REQUIREMENT:

   The facility is needed for the berthing of ships ....

   The mission of the station is ....

(CONTINUED ON DD 1391c)

DD FORM 1391
1 DEC 76

D-1

SAMPLE   Form DD 1391c   **SAMPLE**

1. COMPONENT	FY 2002 MILITARY CONSTRUCTION PROJECT DATA	2. DATE
USMC		05/15/00

3. INSTALLATION AND LOCATION
MARINE CORPS BASE INSTALLATION A

4. PROGRAM ELEMENT	5. PROJECT NUMBER
	IN0215M

11. REQUIREMENT: (CONTINUED)

CURRENT SITUATION:

An adequate facility does not exist to support ....

CORRS rating data.....

Date facility constructed: 1945.

The photographs show the areas were the bulkhead has deteriorated ....

IMPACT IF NOT PROVIDED:

The wharf will continue to deteriorate due to ....

The mission will be impaired due to ....

OTHER NON-PROJECT COSTS:

No collaterial equipment is associated with this project.

No telephone or telecommunications is ....

No audiovisual equipment is ....

ADDITIONAL DATA: *(complete the following items, or indicate if "Not Applicable")*
A.   Facility Number: 1312
B.   Property Record Number: 2-05349
C.   Facility Replacement Cost: $60.0 Million (PRV) *(indicate if PRV or CPV)*
D.   Hazardous Material Information
E.   Economic Analysis: (See attached)
      Economic Alternatives Considered:
          (1) Status Quo: This is not a viable alternative......
          (2) Repair/Modernization: This viable alternative would .....
          (3) Lease: There is no privately owned, commercial, ...
          (4) New Construction: This alternative will construct ......

F.   Other Proposed Projects: MILCON P-234 for upgrading the utilities...

G.   Status of Design: _X_ 35% __ 50% __ 100% __ Final __ Other _____ (Explain)

(CONTINUED ON DD 1391c)

SAMPLE   Form DD 1391c (Cont'd.)   **SAMPLE**

1. COMPONENT	FY 2002 MILITARY CONSTRUCTION PROJECT DATA	2. DATE
USMC		05/15/00

3. INSTALLATION AND LOCATION
MARINE CORPS BASE INSTALLTION A

4. PROGRAM ELEMENT	5. PROJECT NUMBER
	IN0215M

11. REQUIREMENT: (CONTINUED)
ATTACHMENTS:
A. Site plan and vicinity map.
B. Site waivers (e.g: explosive, airfield, etc.).
C. Engineering cost estimate.
D. Economic analysis.
E. Photographs.

12. SIGNATURES:

_____   _____   _____
Responsible Official at Activity   Title   Date

(CONTINUED ON DD 1391c)

DD FORM 1391c
 1 DEC 76

REAL PROPERTY FACILITIES MANUAL

Facilities Projects Documentation Preparation

1. <u>General Information</u>. Facilities projects documentation must be provided on DD Form 1391. Additional data may be continued on DD Form 1391c. The forms are prepared using the procedures outlined in chapter 2. The format is intended to enable the preparing official to systematically provide all important data required for design and/or proper review and validation of the project. It is important that all data be factual and complete so that all projects may be judged on the same basis and receive equitable consideration in approval decisions.

2. <u>Directions</u>. DD Form 1391/1391c, blocks 1 through 12, should be completed in the following:

<u>Block 1. COMPONENT</u>. Enter USMC. FISCAL YEAR. Enter fiscal year assumed in estimate for project execution.

<u>Block 2. DATE</u>. Enter date project was prepared or date project was revised.

<u>Block 3. INSTALLATION AND LOCATION</u>. Enter installation name.

<u>Block 4. PROJECT TITLE</u>. Provide descriptive title of project. Wording should indicate clearly and briefly the type of project and function of the involved facility. Include building or structure number in the title.

<u>Block 5. PROGRAM ELEMENT</u>. Enter type of funds to be used for the project (e.g., O&M,MC).

<u>Block 6. FAC CODE</u>. Enter the four-digit FAC code from DoD Facilities Cost Factors Handbook. If a facility is a multi-use facility, use the FAC code as found on the property record card or the FAC code with the predominant space usage of the facility. Use the new FAC code for a project to convert an existing facility or construct a new facility.

<u>Block 7. PROJECT NUMBER</u>. Enter the project number.

Block 8. PROJECT COST. Enter the estimated project cost. Do not include planning and design cost as part of the project cost unless it is going to be funded under a "design-build" contract. Do not add in SIOH or related costs unless they are an additional cost to the project. Show the planning and design costs on the cost estimate form.

Block 9. COST ESTIMATES. Enter a summary of the project cost estimate in this block including cost of all phases of work. Show the SIOH, contingency, and planning and design cost in this block. The acquisition of equipment (personal property), funded from appropriations for procurement or the capital purchases program, may be shown at the bottom of this block as a non-additive ("NON-ADD") item (i.e., listed as a lump sum with a cost figure in parenthesis).

    a. Column entitled ITEM

       (1) List the primary facility, main building, or structure being repaired or constructed. Estimate includes the cost of built-in equipment normally provided as part of the facility.

       (2) List the supporting facilities items of construction directly related to and required for the support of the primary facility.

       (3) List the subtotal item.

       (4) List contingency if not included in the detailed estimate line items, and any appropriate contract administration.

       (5) List the total funded cost item.

       (6) List the breakdown of items of funded cost for each work classification for combination projects.

       (7) List the total request item.

       (8) List the planning and design cost item.

       (9) List the equipment from other appropriations item.

b. <u>Column entitled U/M</u>. Enter the unit of measure shown in NAVFAC P-72 for each listed item. Lump Sum (LS) may be used only when there is no specific unit of measure available.

c. <u>Column entitled QUANTITY</u>. Enter the quantity for each item.

d. <u>Column entitled UNIT COST</u>. Enter the unit cost in dollars and cents for each item. Lump sum items are shown with a dash.

e. <u>Column entitled COST ($000)</u>. Enter the product of the quantity and unit cost columns rounded to thousands of dollars.

(1) Enter the cost of the primary facility without parenthesis. Components of the primary facility should be entered in parenthesis.

(2) Enter the cost of supporting facilities without parenthesis. Components of the supporting facilities should be entered in parenthesis.

(3) Enter the subtotal cost. The subtotal is the sum of primary facilities and supporting facilities costs (sum of numbers not in parenthesis).

(4) Enter the contingency amount if it is not already included in the detailed estimates line itens and contract administration costs.

(5) Enter the total funded cost. The total funded cost includes the funded cost of all phases of work.

(6) Enter the funded cost for each work classification. Include the costs of all phases for each category of work.

(7) Enter the total request. This cost is the same as total funded cost.

(8) Enter the planning and design cost. This cost will be a funded cost under "design-build" contracts.

(9) Cost of equipment provided from other appropriations should be included in parenthesis.

(10) The total project cost, shown in Block 8, should be the same as total funded cost on the accompanying detailed cost estimate, NAVFAC 11013/7.

Block 10. DESCRIPTION OF PROPOSED CONSTRUCTION. Provide a brief description of the facility condition and proposed work. Indicate the type of construction materials and built-in equipment to be replaced in existing facilities. For projects involving additions, alterations, or conversions, describe the changes to be made.

Block 11. REQUIREMENT. Indicate how much is the "Requirement", and "Adequate" and "Substandard" conditions. This information may be found on the Facility Requirements Plan. Additional information may be continued in DD 1391c.

   a. Project. Provide a brief statement on what the project does.

   b. Requirement. Provide the facts as to why the facility is essential to meet current and/or future operations.

   c. Current Situation. Describe the current situation and how the requirement is presently met. Provide the year when the facility was originally completed and type of construction. If the existing facility is deteriorated or outdated, provide specific information that reflect those conditions, including appropriate CORRS facility condition ratings. If appropriate, provide photographs and small scale drawings.

   d. Impact If Not Provided. Describe the impact, citing the extent and manner of adverse impact on mission accomplishment if the project is not accomplished.

   e. Other Non-Project Costs. Detail the costs of any anxillary collateral equipment, telephone, telecommunciations, audiovisual requirements related to the project.

REAL PROPERTY FACILITIES MANUAL

f. Additional Data

(1) Facility Replacement Cost or PRV from the "Detailed Inventory of Naval Shore Facilities", NAVFAC P-164.

(2) Hazardous Material. Specify the amount, location and cost for asbestos, lead paint and any other hazardous material removal and disposal.

(3) If required, a summary of the options considered in the economic analysis should be listed.

(4) Phasing of a repair project should include the cost of each phase and the fiscal year planned for funding.

(5) Describe any accomplished or proposed military construction or NAF construction, repair and equipment installation project for the facility within the past 24 months and those planned in the next 12 months.

g. Place an X in appropriate design status block.

h. Attachments. List attachments and supporting documentation.

Block 12. SIGNATURES. The commanding officer, staff civil engineer, or public works officer should sign this document as the responsible official. The document should provide the date of signature.

www.ingramcontent.com/pod-product-compliance
Lightning Source LLC
Chambersburg PA
CBHW081115290526
45795CB00006B/2129